OVERCOMING PANIC AND AGORAPHOBIA SELF-HELP COURSE

A 3-part programme based on Cognitive Behavioural Techniques

Part Two: Dealing with Panic Attacks – a self-help manual
Steps 1–3

Derrick Silove

and Vijaya Manicavasagar

ROBINSON
London

Constable & Robinson Ltd
3 The Lanchesters
162 Fulham Palace Road
London W6 9ER
www.overcoming.co.uk

First published in the UK by Robinson,
an imprint of Constable & Robinson Ltd 2006

Important Note
This book is not intended as a substitute for medical advice or treatment.
Any person with a condition requiring medical attention should consult
a qualified medical practitioner or suitable therapist.

ISBN-13: 978-1-84529-439-7 (Pack ISBN)
ISBN-10: 1-84529-439-4

ISBN-13: 978-1-84529-549-3 (Part One)
ISBN-10: 1-84529-549-8

ISBN-13: 978-1-84529-550-9 (Part Two)
ISBN-10: 1-84529-550-1

ISBN-13: 978-1-84529-551-6 (Part Three)
ISBN-10: 1-84529-551-X

1 3 5 7 9 10 8 6 4 2

Printed and bound in the EU

Contents

Introduction: How to Use this Workbook

This is a self-help course for dealing with panic and agoraphobia. It has two aims:

1 To help you develop a better understanding of panic and agoraphobia

2 To teach you practical skills to help you manage and overcome your symptoms

Using a self-help approach

A number of techniques are available to control and manage panic attacks. *The Overcoming Panic and Agoraphobia Self-Help Course* will guide you through some of these skills to help yourself. The course is divided into three parts and offers a first step in combating panic attacks and agoraphobia. You can work through the course on your own or with a friend, or you may like to work with the support of your health-care practitioner or therapist.

What does the course involve?

The three workbooks include a number of questionnaires, charts, worksheets and practical exercises for you to work through. Part One helps you to understand anxiety and panic, and Parts Two and Three set out a six-step self-help course to help you systematically overcome these problems. Part One will probably take two to three weeks to complete, while Parts Two and Three may each take three to four weeks to work through.

It is important to take your time and make sure you are happy with each stage before you move on to the next. There is more detailed information about working through the six-step course provided in Section 1 of this workbook.

Will I benefit from the course?

There are broadly four groups of people who should find this course helpful:

1 People who have panic attacks, with or without agoraphobia, and are interested in learning specific skills to combat anxiety and control panic symptoms and agoraphobia.

2 People who have had panic attacks in the past and who want to learn techniques to prevent the symptoms coming back. Getting to know the early symptoms and how to combat them will help you feel confident about preventing relapse.

3 People who are familiar with the basic principles of anxiety management but who have not incorporated these skills into a structured programme. The skills are likely to be less effective if you use them in a haphazard manner or if you don't practise them regularly.

4 Relatives and friends who want to support you by getting a better understanding of panic disorder and agoraphobia. It's sometimes difficult for the people close to you to know how to help or what to suggest. Getting their support can be very useful, as long as they offer appropriate and constructive advice and support.

What does each part cover?

Part One explains:

- What panic disorder and agoraphobia are
- How panic disorder and agoraphobia affect people's lives
- What causes panic and agoraphobia
- How panic disorder and agoraphobia can be treated
- The defining features of panic attacks, panic disorder and agoraphobia

Part Two explains:

- How to use the six-step course
- Step 1: how to recognize when you are anxious and identify panic triggers
- Step 2: how to change lifestyle factors that contribute to panic attacks
- Step 3: how to control panic attacks

Part Three explains:

- Step 4: how to challenge unhelpful thinking styles
- Step 5: how to deal with physical sensations

- Step 6: how to overcome agoraphobia and troubleshoot problem areas

- How to prevent setbacks

How to get the most from the course

Here are some tips to help you get the most from the course:

- These workbooks are practical tools – you don't need to keep the pages pristine. Use the space provided to complete the exercises, and feel free to use the pages to jot down any thoughts or notes, or highlight anything that's particularly useful. This will keep all of your notes in one place, which will be helpful when you come to read back through them later on.

- Keep an open mind and be willing to experiment with new ideas and skills. These workbooks will sometimes ask you to think about painful issues. This may be difficult, but if anxiety, panic and agoraphobia are restricting your life it's worth making the effort to overcome these problems – the rewards will be substantial.

- It's important to commit to the course to get the most out of it – so set aside up to half an hour each day to complete the practical exercises.

- Try to answer all of the questions and complete all of the exercises, even if you have to come back to some of them later. There may be times when you get stuck and can't think of how to take things forward. If this happens, don't get angry with yourself or give up. Just put the workbook aside and come back to it later, when you're feeling more relaxed.

- You may find it helpful to have the support of a friend – two heads are often better than one. And if both of you are working through the course you may be able to encourage each other to carry on, even when one of you is finding it hard.

- Use the 'Thoughts and Reflections' section at the back of each workbook to write down anything that you find particularly helpful.

- Reread the workbooks. You may get more out of them once you've had a chance to think about some of the ideas and put them into practice.

- The course is designed so that each workbook builds on what has already been covered – for instance, what you learn in Part One will help you when you come to Part Two. While you can dip into the different sections of Part One, it's important to work through the six-step course in Parts Two and Three systematically. Don't progress to the next step until you've practised and mastered the previous one. It doesn't matter how long it takes you to work through the six steps – what's most important is to understand the techniques and practise the skills.

When should you seek further assistance?

Some people with symptoms of panic may need more help and support than these workbooks can provide. If you fall into one of the seven categories described below, it's likely that you'll benefit from the help of a doctor or therapist:

1 People who have any of the rare physical conditions that mimic panic attacks – described in Section 3 of Part One. It's important to consult your doctor if you suspect that you may have one of these conditions.

2 People with severe agoraphobia – especially if it is unrelated to symptoms of panic. These workbooks are for people suffering primarily from panic disorder, who may or may not have some degree of agoraphobia.

3 People with severe depression associated with panic disorder, who might not have the motivation to work through a self-help book on their own. There's a brief guide to managing depression after this introduction.

4 People who lack the confidence to work on their own, or who feel that a self-help course isn't enough. It's important to be fully motivated to follow this course – if you practise the techniques half-heartedly you're unlikely to get good results.

5 People with a strong resistance to making changes in their life.

6 People who have panic attacks and agoraphobia as only one aspect of wider emotional, social or personality problems. For example, if you respond to stress by misusing drugs or alcohol, you may need to seek counselling for substance abuse before (or at the same time as) trying to overcome panic disorder.

7 People with severe mental health issues – for example people who are severely depressed or have psychosis. In these cases it's important to seek the help of a mental health professional.

A Note on Depression

It's quite common for depression and anxiety to go hand in hand. But if you have panic disorder it's unlikely that you'll feel depressed all of the time – it's more usual for these feelings to be fleeting or relatively minor. It might be that you feel depressed for a short while because you've experienced a setback or that you're having to cope with more everyday stress than you've been used to for a while. Some people experience a few days of depressed mood following a panic attack.

As long as you feel positive about life most of the time, it's likely that you'll be able to sustain your energy and motivation to continue learning and practising the techniques to help you overcome panic attacks and agoraphobia. But if you find that you're depressed all or most of the time, and this feeling becomes overwhelming, it's time to get some professional help.

How to deal with minor depression

You can use a self-help approach to combat minor bouts of depression that last a few hours or days. Try these steps:

- Write a list of the stressors that are making you feel depressed, and use the problem-solving technique you learnt in Step 6 to work through any problems.

- Use the techniques in Step 3 to focus your mind on things that you enjoy or which give you pleasure. This is a good approach if you can't easily deal with whatever's making you feel depressed.

- Negative thinking can make you feel depressed. So take another look at Step 4, where you learnt how to identify and challenge negative thinking, and substitute these unhelpful thoughts with more positive and constructive ones.

Dealing with depression

Write down the stressors you face and try to work out step-by-step strategies to deal with them

Do something that helps raise your self-esteem – engage in an activity that's pleasurable and non-stressful

Examine whether your thoughts about yourself, your situation and the future are excessively negative. Challenge these negative thoughts and try to replace them with helpful ones

If your symptoms persist, or if you feel desperate and you're unable to cope, seek professional help

Regular counselling sessions and/or medication   Hospitalization

It's important to get some professional help if these self-help techniques don't make you feel better, or you start to feel hopeless or desperate. Don't try to battle it out yourself – there's lots of support available if you ask for help.

Your doctor may suggest an antidepressant medicine and/or regular counselling sessions to help you get through your depression. If you're severely depressed, you may need intensive treatment such as a stay in hospital – being looked after like this can help your recovery and protect you from neglecting or harming yourself and eventually put you back on the road to recovery.

SECTION 1: Introducing the Six-Step Self-Help Course

This section will help you understand:

- The early hurdles to self-help

- The importance of committing to change

- Dealing with setbacks

- How you can undermine your own efforts

- How to use the six-step self-help course

- When it's normal to feel anxious

This course should give you the basic skills to control panic attacks and overcome agoraphobia. It is supported by several years of research and clinical experience, which demonstrates that these techniques are effective.

Early hurdles to self-help

There are a number of techniques to control and even eliminate panic attacks, and you can use the *Overcoming Panic and Agoraphobia Self-Help Course* to learn these skills to help yourself. To get the best from the course, it's useful to understand the things that can undermine your efforts. Two of the most important are:

1 Fear of change

The six-step course suggests ways of changing aspects of your life that cause and perpetuate panic attacks and agoraphobia. Making changes to your lifestyle and your daily routine can seem daunting. It may feel safer to keep things as they are – but even though the thought of changing things might make you feel more anxious temporarily, it's important to confront the reality. Although the limitations in your lifestyle – like avoiding going to the city or taking a train – may make life more 'comfortable', these restrictions can be extremely disabling in the long term. They can affect relationships with your family and friends, and stop you enjoying the things that other people take for granted.

2 Lack of support

You might want to tell your friends and relatives that you're following this self-help course, but be prepared for some of them to be unenthusiastic or discouraging. They might even be dismissive and express disbelief that a book can really help, but this could be because the people close to you are overly cautious or protective. They may also be worried that once your condition improves, they might have to start making changes to their own lives – this could take effort and involve doing things that make them feel uncomfortable.

Whatever the reason for their lack of support, it's important to realize that the choice to change is your own decision. It can be helpful to have the support of your friends and family while you're following this course, but it's not critical to your success.

Committing to change

Before you start the course it's useful to think about the potential benefits and drawbacks of overcoming panic attacks and agoraphobia. This will help you see how making changes to your life can be a positive experience, even though it might be rather scary. Here's an exercise to help you work out how making changes – or not – might impact on your life.

Make a list of the pros and cons of making these changes and rate each from −10 to +10 in terms of its importance in improving your lifestyle. It might help to focus on the reasons for making the changes.

- A '−' score indicates that you feel the lifestyle change will have a negative impact.

- A score of '0' indicates that the change will have 'no effect on your lifestyle' or a 'neutral' effect.

- A '+' score indicates that the change will be beneficial.

Working out the benefits of change: *example*

Benefits of change	Impact on lifestyle (−10 to +10)	Consequence of no change	Impact on lifestyle (−10 to +10)
Able to go to supermarket alone	+7	Have to wait for friend/mother to go out with me	−3
Able to find a job	+9	Forced to stay at home and watch TV	−5
Able to go to the movies with friends	+5	Have to wait for video or DVD version to be released	−4
Could throw a dinner party	+8	Can't socialize with groups of friends	−4

Now complete the table below with as many examples as you can think of:

Working out the benefits of change

Benefits of change	Impact on lifestyle (−10 to +10)	Consequence of no change	Impact on lifestyle (−10 to +10)

Making a list of the benefits of change can be helpful because it's a good reminder of why it's so important to overcome panic attacks and agoraphobia. In addition, rereading your list is an easy way to renew your motivation along the way – at times when the effort to change seems too great, or if you've had a temporary setback in your course.

It's important to think of overcoming panic attacks as worthwhile and necessary – and as important as any other commitment, such as your career, studying for a qualification or caring for your family. There's no 'magic cure' or a 'fast-acting pill' that will immediately get rid of your anxiety symptoms. If it were that easy, you wouldn't be reading this book! Beating panic disorder and/or agoraphobia requires time, some hard work and a determination to succeed. The key to success is to:

- Treat each small success as a step towards overcoming the problem

- Accept that there may be small setbacks along the way

Dealing with setbacks

Setbacks can happen in any treatment programme, and at the beginning it can be difficult to control all sources of stress and all triggers of panic attacks. Sometimes you might find that a number of small stressors occur in rapid succession, which makes it difficult to keep on track with the course and make changes to your daily life.

On top of that, a single major life event, such as the death of a family member or a close friend being seriously ill, may cause your panic attacks and agoraphobia to return. Setbacks can also occur and cause anxiety symptoms to flare up when you're tired or under the weather – for example if you're too busy at work, having a run of poor sleep, or when you're recovering from the flu. It becomes harder to control your symptoms if these stressors occur before you've mastered the anxiety-management skills you're learning.

The important thing is how you deal with these minor setbacks – you'll make the best progress if you keep a positive attitude, put any setbacks down to experience, then simply try again:

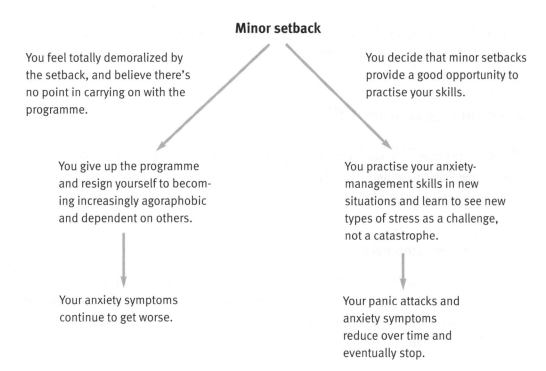

Minor setback

You feel totally demoralized by the setback, and believe there's no point in carrying on with the programme.

You decide that minor setbacks provide a good opportunity to practise your skills.

You give up the programme and resign yourself to becoming increasingly agoraphobic and dependent on others.

You practise your anxiety-management skills in new situations and learn to see new types of stress as a challenge, not a catastrophe.

Your anxiety symptoms continue to get worse.

Your panic attacks and anxiety symptoms reduce over time and eventually stop.

The urge to quit

It's likely that you'll feel like quitting on several occasions during the course. Falling back on the same, safe routines – however restrictive they are – may seem more comfortable than keeping up the effort it takes to make the changes.

If you feel the urge to quit, try one or more of the following to get you back on track:

- Read through your 'benefits of change' table to remind yourself that it is worth continuing.

- Talk to a close, supportive friend or relative about the benefits of overcoming anxiety – again, this will help to remind you about the reasons for continuing.

- Accept that a break in the course is not a disaster and doesn't mean you've failed. Try returning to an earlier step when you feel ready to begin again.

- Recognize that you may have tried to work through the course too quickly – you might not have given yourself enough time to practise the skills introduced in the earlier stages. Try doing more practice, and allow yourself more time to complete each step – this can help consolidate what you've learnt.

- Visualize or imagine a panic-free lifestyle and think about all the things you'll be able to do without the old restrictions – this will help motivate you to continue.

Undermining your own efforts

You may find that you ask yourself the same self-defeating questions – like the two below – over and over again, and this can undermine your confidence. Spend some time thinking about this before you begin the course.

Why can't I just stop panicking?

This is a common question for people with panic disorder, but you can't just 'decide' not to panic any more – it's not a question of willpower. The stresses that lead to your first panic attack can build up over many months or years, even though it may have seemed like your first attack came out of the blue.

The build up to panic attacks:

- Your body's physiological processes gradually adapt to your rising tension levels.

- Once the 'habit' of triggering panic has set in, it takes time to reset your body's mechanisms to a normal level, where the underlying degree of tension is not so close to the 'fight or flight' trigger.

- Your body needs to be physically 'realigned' to the way it was before you started to adapt to your rising tension levels.

If you or the people around you expect that you can stop your panic attacks by willpower, you can feel unnecessary pressure to get better quickly. Unfortunately, trying to manage your attacks by sheer effort of will alone, without the skills to apply the necessary techniques, does not automatically guarantee success. It can be disappointing if you don't recover immediately – and blaming yourself only creates extra pressure. This added pressure can then fuel further panic attacks and make you feel even more demoralized.

If you've had a panic attack, you're probably sure to remember what the first episode felt like, even years later. It's a powerful experience that usually makes you more sensitive to any sensations that remind you of that first attack. It's difficult and unhelpful to try to forget your first experience of panic – what's important is to try to place those memories in the past, where they are no longer threatening.

Repeated panic attacks undermine your self-confidence, so that after a run of them you become unsure of yourself and worry about doing something embarrassing when you're with other people. Things that once seemed easy – such as driving through heavy traffic, waiting for a bus or buying tickets to a movie – become major ordeals. You might find that you're relying on other people too much, or you may begin to feel isolated and incompetent. It's important to remember:

- It takes time and patience to regain your self-confidence as you slowly attempt to overcome your anxiety in different situations.

- As with most practical tasks that take practice, you'll succeed with some attempts, while others may be disappointing.

- Eventually, as you accomplish more tasks successfully, your self-confidence will improve, but the process is a gradual one.

Why am I different?

You may notice that your relationships with the people close to you have changed since you began to have panic attacks. Unfortunately, some of these changes may not be healthy or satisfying:

- You might notice that your partner, children or friends treat you differently because you may find it distressing to leave the house or take part in social activities.

- Some friends may even desert you because you don't want to join in with the things they want to do.

- Relatives might offer simple and thoughtless 'advice', or even try to bully you into overcoming your anxiety and avoidance behaviour.

When you've learnt how to manage your anxiety, and your panic attacks have subsided, you might notice that your relationships with other people have become stuck – they continue to treat you as if you still have panic disorder. For instance, your family and friends may have reorganized aspects of their own lifestyles to accommodate yours, so it will take time and patience to re-educate them to behave differently.

Not all of the after-effects of recovering from panic disorder are negative:

- You're likely to be more sensitive to other people's distress and tension and better able to understand their difficulties and anxieties.

- You'll probably be able to suggest techniques and skills to help your family and friends to control their anxiety.

- Many of the skills you've learnt and used to overcome panic attacks and agora-phobia can be applied to other stress-related problems. And you can call on these skills when you need to deal with other stressful events later in life.

About the self-help course

Not all of the skills presented in the course will be appropriate for everyone, but most people will find at least some of them helpful. Even if you think that a particular exercise or approach won't work for you, it's important to try it and practise the technique for some time before you decide whether or not it has been useful. Remember that anxiety-management techniques, like most skills, take time to learn and you may not see the benefits immediately.

- It's likely to take about six to eight weeks to complete the course, but this is only a rough guide.

- You'll get the most from the course if you work systematically through the six steps.

- Don't progress to the next step until you've practised and mastered the previous ones.

- It is important not to work through the course as fast as possible but to understand the techniques and to practise the skills, no matter how long it takes.

CASE STUDY: Joan

'I kept surprising myself how easy it was to do the things that I previously feared. There were so many changes in my lifestyle once I started going out again. I could drive around, visit my friends, pick up the kids from school and go shopping. Best of all, I could start looking for a job, something I've always wanted to do but couldn't consider because of my panic attacks. My relationship with my husband has improved because we don't fight like we used to about my reliance on him. I've even started going out to the club with my girlfriends every Wednesday night. I really feel like I'm living again.'

How to use the six-step course

The best approach is to:

- Skim through the six steps in Part Two and Part Three to get an idea of the skills and tasks involved. This will make the whole course seem more manageable and should reduce any anxiety you're feeling about what lies ahead.

- Once you're more familiar with the books, work through each of the six steps in turn. First, read through a section to the end without completing the exercises. Then go back to the beginning of the section and attempt the suggested tasks or exercises.

- Make sure that you've grasped each step and you're comfortable practising the techniques it introduces before you move on to the next one.

- When you've worked through the six steps systematically, you may want to re-read your workbooks to reinforce the skills you've learnt.

Getting the support of a friend or relative

It's often easier to work on a project with someone else, so you could try asking a friend or relative to help you through the six-step course. If you like this sort of approach, it might make all the difference – working with a partner can:

- Be a good way to make sure that you practise the skills.

- Keep you motivated to work through the whole course.

- Support you through the difficult times, when you may be tempted to give up, or you become temporarily discouraged.

- Help you to acknowledge your successes, especially when you may not recognize them as significant achievements yourself.

On the other hand, there will come a point when you need to carry out the tasks and exercises on your own to make a full recovery. You need to recognize this and talk it through with your helper in advance. It's important to discuss this issue regularly with each other, so that you don't delay the point at which you are ready to work independently.

The six steps

Here's an overview of the six steps of the self-help course:

Step 1 – you will get to know how you react to stress – what symptoms you have – and how to identify the 'triggers' that set off your panic attacks. This step focuses on learning to keep an eye on your symptoms so that you'll be able to tell the difference between actual anxiety symptoms and other symptoms that seem like anxiety but are really due to other factors.

Step 2 – you'll focus on the lifestyle factors that can increase the risk of panic attacks. In particular, you'll look at the importance of diet, exercise, sleep and relaxation to your psychological health.

Step 3 – this introduces some specific techniques to control panic attacks and other anxiety symptoms when they occur. If you're able to control these symptoms, you'll increase your self-confidence and begin to tackle situations that you may have been avoiding.

Step 4 – will look at the negative thinking patterns that may be contributing to your anxiety symptoms. There's little doubt that our attitudes and thoughts about ourselves, our bodily sensations and outside events can influence the way we feel and behave. Changing some of these attitudes makes it possible to change the way we feel about ourselves, our lives and our feelings – which can influence our levels of anxiety and stress.

Step 5 – examines how physical sensations trigger fearful thinking, increasing the risk of further panic. By understanding and labelling your physical sensations more accurately, you'll be able to reduce this type of thinking.

Step 6 – focuses on applying the skills you've learnt in a wide range of situations to overcome agoraphobia and establish a healthy lifestyle. Learning to control anxiety and to overcome panic disorder means more than just keeping symptoms at bay: it eventually means enjoying your life to the full, rather than constantly focusing on the fear of having another panic attack.

There's a review section at the end of each step, which will help you to monitor your improvement and set the pace for further progress. You might find that you need to re-read certain sections or reattempt some exercises before you move on to the next step.

Step 1. *Recognizing when you are anxious and identifying panic triggers*
(learning accurately to monitor physical and psychological symptoms of panic
and sources of stress)

Step 2. *Lifestyle factors that may be contributing to anxiety and panic attacks*
(changing aspects of lifestyle to reduce the likelihood of panic attacks occurring)

Step 3. *Controlling panic attacks*
(learning techniques to control and eliminate panic attacks)

Step 4. *Changing unhelpful thinking styles*
(identifying, challenging and learning to change negative thinking styles)

Step 5. *Reducing sensitivity to physical sensations*
(learning to not be fearful of 'normal' physical sensations)

Step 6. *Putting these skills into practice*
(overcoming panic and agoraphobia and establishing a new lifestyle)

When it's normal to feel anxious

It may be helpful to think about the following points before you start working
through the six steps. You might also find it useful to read this section again as you
work through each of the six steps.

Normal anxiety and panic

This course will help you to stop having panic attacks in everyday situations such as
shopping, driving or waiting your turn at a bank. But there are some situations where
sensations identical to panic are entirely normal. For example, some fairground rides

such as the roller-coaster or Big Dipper excite people by producing feelings which are very similar to panic but which are enjoyable – for some!

It's also normal to feel heightened tension in testing situations such as during examinations or when you're giving a presentation – in fact this feeling helps you to perform at your best. And it's normal to feel symptoms of arousal and fear in situations where your life is threatened, such as being caught up in a bank robbery or being involved in a car accident. This is part of the 'fight or flight response' discussed earlier.

Some situations will still evoke these powerful emotions, even after you've mastered all the techniques for controlling panic attacks and eliminating anxiety symptoms. It's worth bearing this in mind: your goal is not to stop feeling anxious in all situations. So it's important to set realistic goals in managing your anxiety and in overcoming panic attacks.

Preventing anxiety and panic attacks from developing

It's often easier to stop a panic attack when it is in its early stages than to try to bring it to an end when it's already in full swing. At the first sign of panic, it's important to apply the techniques you've learnt without delay. In time, and with regular practice, you'll find that these skills will kick in almost automatically, and it will become increasingly easier to control the symptoms before they escalate.

A final note

Try to always keep in mind that you are doing the six-step course for yourself, for your future lifestyle and for the people you care about. It's likely that there will be several times during the course when your motivation disappears and you feel like giving up. When you experience these low periods, try to keep in mind all the positive changes to your lifestyle and to your relationships that you'll gain from overcoming panic disorder and agoraphobia.

Summary

- A fear of change and a lack of support are two of the early hurdles you may have to deal with when you start the six-step course. It's important to focus on the 'gains' you'll make from overcoming your problems, and acknowledge that it will take effort to make the changes and that this may feel uncomfortable at first.

- It's important to be fully committed to the course – focus on the potential benefits of making these life changes, and the drawbacks you'll experience if you don't tackle your anxiety symptoms.

- You're likely to experience setbacks, but it's important to pick yourself up and dust yourself off. You might also feel an urge to quit. Keep a positive attitude and carry on practising the new skills you're learning. It might help to go back to the previous step in the course to make sure your new skills are bedded in properly.

- You may try to undermine your own efforts by thinking that you can overcome your problems by willpower alone. Other people may suggest this as well. But remember that it's very unlikely that you'll be able to will yourself to be less anxious. It takes time and patience to reprogramme your body to a normal level of anxiety, and to regain your self-confidence.

- Take as much time as you need to complete the six-step course – it's not a race. Read through each step before you embark on it, to familiarize yourself with the exercises you're about to do. You might also want to ask a friend or relative to support you as you work through the course.

SECTION 2: Step 1 – Identifying Your Panic Triggers

This section will help you understand:

- What your symptoms mean
- How to identify your panic triggers

What do your symptoms mean?

If you've experienced anxiety for as long as you can remember, you're probably something of an expert when it comes to knowing the symptoms. But it's easy to confuse feeling anxious with the symptoms of a serious illness because they can have such similar effects on your body. And worrying that you're ill makes you feel anxious – it's a vicious circle.

Some people who have panic attacks often think that their chest pains or breathlessness mean that they're having a heart attack – it's difficult to believe that being anxious can produce such serious symptoms. It's even more confusing when you're not aware of the stresses that cause your anxiety symptoms – it's this that seems to make some panic attacks feel like they come 'out of the blue'. And it only reinforces the worry that your symptoms are due to a physical illness.

Common symptoms of panic disorder:	Common thoughts that these symptoms produce:
Tightness in the chest	'I'm having a heart attack'
Difficulty breathing	'I'm having a stroke'
Strange feelings of unreality	'I've got a brain tumour'

You might have experienced these symptoms and visited your doctor for tests and a check up – cardiac stress tests and numerous blood tests for instance – to try to find a physical cause for your symptoms. In fact it's not uncommon for people having a panic attack to be admitted to hospital for a suspected heart attack.

Pinpointing the symptoms of panic

So how do you know when you're experiencing symptoms of panic rather than a physical illness? When you visit your doctor, he or she will diagnose your illness by identifying several symptoms that are known to occur together in a regular pattern. You probably tend to recognize your emotions in a similar way – for example if you're feeling down and you're crying, you might 'diagnose' that you're upset or sad. Here are some other examples:

Symptoms		Emotion
Flushed face		
Clenched jaw	⟶	Anger
Shallow breathing		
Hostile thoughts		
Poor concentration		
Preoccupation with pessimistic thoughts		Depression
Disturbed sleep	⟶	
Lack of energy		

Everyone experiences their feelings in different ways, and to different degrees. Your own pattern probably varies slightly, depending on the situation you're in. But when your emotional state develops into a serious problem, it's likely that your particular pattern of symptoms will become consistent enough to pinpoint panic disorder, for instance.

Exercise 1

Think about the general pattern of symptoms that you've experienced in the past when you felt despondent or depressed. Write down a list of these symptoms in the space below:

Your pattern of symptoms when you are depressed:

1 —————————————   4 —————————————

2 —————————————   5 —————————————

3 —————————————   6 —————————————

You can do the same exercise for anxiety, to get an idea of the common patterns of symptoms that you experience when you're stressed or anxious. Think back to the last time you felt really anxious and panicky and write down a list of the major symptoms:

Your major symptoms of panic:

1 ————————————————   4 ————————————————

2 ————————————————   5 ————————————————

3 ————————————————   6 ————————————————

Once you've completed the second list, think back to the last three times you experienced that group of symptoms. On each occasion, did you think you were suffering from a physical illness at the time? Were you baffled by the symptoms, or did you immediately put them down to being anxious? Write down the three occasions in the first column of the table below, and note how you felt under each of the other headings:

Monitoring your symptoms of panic			
Occasion	Did you think you had a physical illness?	Were you baffled by the symptoms?	Did you recognize that these were symptoms of anxiety?

The next time you experience these symptoms together, try to remember that they are symptoms of anxiety rather than a sign that you've got a serious physical illness. Simply thinking this thought – that you're not actually physically ill – can help you to feel less anxious.

Identifying and monitoring panic triggers

It's worth monitoring your panic attacks while you're following this course so that you can identify your major panic triggers. You can do this by keeping a diary of your panic attacks – there's an example below – noting down when and where each attack happens and what the trigger seemed to be.

Exercise 2

- In your diary, give each attack a rating between 0 and 10, where:

'0' indicates 'minimal symptoms'

'10' indicates the 'worst possible symptoms'.

- You may also find it useful to rate your level of coping with each panic attack. Use a similar rating scale, where:

'0' indicates the 'poorest level of coping'

'10' indicates your 'best or most effective level of coping'.

If you like, you can use the final column to write down how you would have liked to cope with each particular situation.

	Example of diary entries for monitoring panic attacks			
Date	Situation	Anxious symptoms (0–10)	Coping (0–10)	How I would have liked to cope
4 May	At sister's house with her family	7	4 Had to leave the room	Stayed in the room to cope
12 May	Waiting in line at the bank	8	2 Left the bank in a hurry	Kept my place in the queue
6 June	Taking the dog for a walk	5	6 Managed to complete the walk	Completed the walk without being anxious
10 June	Speaking to my mother on the telephone: I felt criticized	6	7 Continued talking but could not concentrate	Told my mother I felt criticized, so I could hold my concentration

Panic attack diary

Date	Situation	Anxious symptoms (0-10)	Coping (0-10)	How I would have liked to cope

These are some common situations where people have panic attacks:

- Driving a car

- Taking public transport

- Visiting a busy shopping centre

- Attending a social function

You may find that there are other situations that you regularly find stressful. Your anxiety can also be very specific: for example, you may feel anxious in the company of some people but not others. Note down as much detail as possible in your diary so that you can start to see if there are any patterns to your anxiety.

Use this diary to monitor your panic attacks over the next few weeks. (There is an extra blank copy of the form, and of the other forms used in later steps of the course, at the back of the book.) When you rate your level of anxiety, it's important to recognize what's a 'normal' range of anxiety. Some situations make most people feel anxious, such as going for a job interview or giving a presentation. Try discussing your level of anxiety with someone else so that you develop a realistic picture of the types of situations that make most people feel anxious.

Common sources of anxiety

When you describe situations in which you feel anxious, try to be as specific as possible. This will help you to pinpoint particular types of situations that seem to trigger your panic attacks. You'll probably find that you can group together a number of situations because they share certain characteristics or trigger particular fears. Some of these common features are listed below – see how many you find familiar:

- **Escape not possible** Feeling trapped – being unable to escape easily from a situation – can trigger intense anxiety symptoms and panic attacks for people with panic disorder. Lots of people find that crowded places such as shopping centres, sports stadiums or restaurants make them anxious.

- **Embarrassment** If you have panic attacks you may be particularly sensitive to other people seeing you panic. Once the panic symptoms start, it can make you feel even more anxious if you think people are looking at you. Sometimes this extra 'layer' of anxiety is enough to trigger a full-blown panic attack.

- **Help not available** People with panic disorder need to feel that 'help' is close by in case they have a panic attack. You might find, for instance, that your anxiety subsides when you're with a friend or relative, or when you're somewhere that you can get help, such as a hospital or a doctor's surgery.

- **'Going crazy'** When you start to have a panic attack you might think that the symptoms will just get worse and worse until you faint, 'go crazy' or have a heart attack. These catastrophic thoughts make you feel more anxious and tend to make the symptoms worse – which can make the attack last longer or trigger another one.

- **Losing control** With the symptoms it produces, it's not surprising that a panic attack makes you feel like you're losing control. This fear may be so strong that you truly believe you're about to lose control over your behaviour, hurt someone or act in a bizarre and embarrassing way. And if you're in a crowded place it only makes things worse because there are people around who would see this happening. In reality you're not going to harm other people or act dangerously. But the fear that this might happen – along with fear of embarrassment – can make you particularly anxious about certain situations.

Exercise 3

Use the table overleaf to identify the triggers that make your anxiety symptoms worse in particular situations. For example, if you feel anxious when you go shopping with friends, write this situation in the first column, and tick the 'embarrassment' column if that's what makes you feel anxious.

Monitoring situations that trigger common fears

Situation	Escape not possible	Embarrassment	Help not available	Going crazy/fear of collapse

Identifying and monitoring agoraphobic symptoms

Exercise 4

You may find that you're actually avoiding situations or entering certain situations only with great reluctance because of your anxiety. Are there any situations or activities that you've been avoiding? List them in the table below (again, there is an extra table at the back of this workbook). When you've completed the list, rate each of these situations or activities on a scale of '0' to '10', in terms of the difficulty you experience on approaching or entering them, where:

- '0' indicates 'no anxiety' or 'no difficulty'
- '10' indicates 'extreme anxiety' or 'severe difficulty'.

Monitoring situations or activities that you may be avoiding	
Situation	Anxiety rating (0–10)

Summary

Review of Step 1

When you've monitored your panic attacks and avoidance behaviour for a few days, you should be able to spot any patterns emerging. Once you've identified these patterns, you'll be able to focus on applying your anxiety-management skills to these situations. In time, knowing when to use these skills to cope with a particular situation will help you to overcome panic attacks and agoraphobia.

Exercise 1

For this exercise, you wrote down the pattern of symptoms you experience when you become depressed. Next you wrote down your pattern of symptoms when you become anxious. Looking back at the lists, try to answer these questions:

1 Could you detect a specific pattern of symptoms?

2 Can you list all the symptoms you experience?

Next time you experience some or all of these symptoms, try to say to yourself 'These sensations probably mean that I am anxious' rather than jumping to the conclusion that you've got a serious physical illness, you're going 'crazy', or you're about to collapse.

Summary continues on next page

Summary

Exercise 2

This exercise tried to help you identify what types of situations and associated fears are likely to trigger a panic attack. Looking back at your panic attack diary, try to answer these questions:

3 Do your panic attacks tend to occur at particular times of the day or night?

4 Are there particular situations that are more difficult for you than others?

By monitoring your panic attacks, you'll be able to focus on some of the things that could be making you feel anxious. For example, if you tend to have panic attacks at the end of the day, it could be that you're more likely to have them when you're tired. If you tend to have attacks at night, you may be dwelling on the day's worries before you go to sleep, or drinking too much tea or coffee before you go to bed. If you drink a lot of alcohol, it's also possible that you're experiencing withdrawal symptoms from alcohol misuse during the night.

Summary continues on next page

Summary

Exercise 3

This exercise tried to help you become aware of the situations that could make your symptoms worse. You noted down the situations that are most likely to trigger fearful thinking. Looking back at your checklist for monitoring situations that trigger common fears, try to answer these questions:

5 Do you tend to have specific fears and worries in certain situations? What are they?

We'll look in detail at ways of overcoming these fears and worries in Step 4, but it's helpful to become aware of them early in the programme so that you can begin to confront them.

Exercise 4

This exercise helped to highlight any situations that you avoid and asked you to rate the severity of your symptoms in those situations. By rating your responses in this way, you'll be able to set yourself realistic targets to try to confront your fears. By working through the list slowly, from the easiest to the most difficult, over the course of this programme, you'll gradually be able to overcome your need to avoid these situations.

Remember:

Fix a time each week – write it on your calendar to make sure you remember – to review your progress and your monitoring forms. Make sure that you've been using all of the Step 1 monitoring forms for at least a week before you move on to Step 2. This next step focuses on lifestyle factors that may be contributing to your panic attacks.

SECTION 3: Step 2 – Changing Your Lifestyle

This section will help you understand:

- How stress is linked to anxiety
- The mind-body link
- How to improve your physical health
- How to relax

Life stress and anxiety: a vicious cycle

Having a stressful lifestyle can play a part in anxiety symptoms and panic attacks if you're susceptible to them. If you have panic attacks, it's likely that you'll be able to remember several stressful incidents – perhaps a particularly busy project at work, or a member of your family being ill – that happened just before the attacks began. And some of these stresses may have continued or got worse once your attacks started.

When you're having panic attacks it's often more difficult to solve stressful problems because of the added energy it takes to cope with the anxiety you're feeling. This can become a vicious cycle of life stress and anxiety, where life stress makes your panic symptoms worse. They, in turn, make you feel even more stressed, which makes you more susceptible to panic attacks.

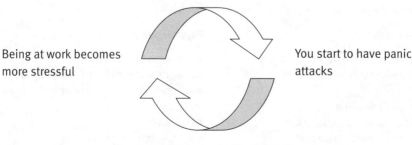

You attempt to solve a backlog at work by putting in more hours, skipping meals and not exercising

Being at work becomes more stressful

You start to have panic attacks

You become increasingly anxious about having a panic attack at work

You might find that you're locked into a similar cycle if you've started to argue or have difficulties with your spouse or partner since you began to have panic attacks. The added stress on your relationship can make your panic attacks worse, which then puts even more pressure on the relationship. If you start having trouble sleeping, or you avoid going out with your friends, this extra stress just increases your tension levels even further.

These everyday stressors can slow down your recovery from panic disorder, especially if you don't know how to manage your symptoms. And if your lifestyle itself is also stressful – say you're always eating on the run, rather than sitting down to enjoy a proper meal, or you don't take time out to relax and enjoy yourself – it can have the same effect. Not getting enough sleep can also have a big impact.

It's almost impossible to avoid all sources of stress while you recover from panic disorder, so it's important to set yourself a realistic goal. The best approach is to solve problems where you can and learn how to become more resilient to things that are outside your control – such as a close friend being seriously ill. Many problems can be solved though, and you'll learn some useful problem-solving techniques in Step 6 of this course.

Step 2 is about building up your resilience to everyday stressors such as tension at work. You'll learn how to make some simple lifestyle changes to lower your vulnerability to panic attacks. There are four areas that are vital in reducing anxiety and in overcoming panic attacks:

- Exercise
- Sleep
- Nutrition
- Relaxation

Types of stress: the mind-body link

There are two main types of stress – mental stress and physical stress:

Mental stress	Physical stress
This is characterized by fears and worries. You may worry excessively about: • Work • Your family or friends • Having another panic attack, coping with public transport, or waiting in line	This relates to your physical health, and makes you more susceptible to fatigue, minor illnesses and irritability – all the ingredients of being 'run down': • Your diet • Not taking enough exercise • Not getting enough sleep

If you're feeling 'run down' or you're physically unfit, you can be more vulnerable to other stressors, so you're more likely to feel tired and have headaches and tense muscles. And because your mind and body are so closely linked, feeling tired or ill can 'feed back' in a circular fashion, and affect your mental health – a stress cycle:

BODY
(symptoms include stomach upsets,
muscle tension and headaches)

MIND
(symptoms include fears and worries,
poor self-esteem and loss of confidence)

For example, if you're feeling run down and haven't slept well for several days, you're more likely to feel irritable and might not be able to concentrate properly. This can affect your self-esteem and confidence, which can then make you feel more anxious and depressed. Some people find that this kind of physical stress is all it takes to trigger a panic attack.

You may have noticed that when you've just got over the flu, or some other physical illness, it takes a bit of time to get back to your usual self – you feel 'down', exhausted or stressed. This is why it's so important to rest properly when you're ill. If you don't take time to recharge your batteries, by taking time off from your usual daily tasks and activities, you'll feel physically stressed for longer. This can impact on your psychological state. You need to learn to make time for yourself – to look after your physical and mental health. But even doing this can be a challenge in itself.

Simply recognizing the link between your mind and body can help you to prepare to reduce your stress levels. And just as chronic physical fatigue can make you more vulnerable to stress, improving your physical health can make you more resistant to stressful situations. Have you noticed that when you've had a good night's sleep and a healthy breakfast, it's much easier to take on the world – you perform better at work and your daily chores seem much less of an effort. Even being hungry can make it difficult to concentrate – think about that last half hour of work before lunch.

How to target your physical health

This section targets four main problem areas for physical stress: exercise, nutrition, sleep and relaxation. Even if you always get a good night's sleep, or go for a long walk every day, it's important to make sure you're focusing on all of the areas so that you reduce your vulnerability to stress.

Exercise

Regular exercise – even if it's just a daily walk – can make it easier to cope, mentally, with the stresses of life. It's a good way to:

- 'Work off' tension and monotony, especially if you spend most of your day at your desk or you don't move about much

- Get a better night's sleep

- Meet people

- Add a bit of variety to your day

You could think about joining an exercise club or gym, or going for a swim or playing tennis. Meeting a new group of people can take your mind off your worries and it's a good way to direct your attention away from your anxiety symptoms.

The type of exercise you choose, and whether you do it alone, with a friend or as part of a team, depends on the types of exercise you like doing, your physical make-up and your level of stamina. You might find that it's more fun to exercise with a friend and it's a great way to keep you going on days when your motivation is low.

When you start to exercise make sure you choose something that you enjoy and you'll be able to stick with, rather than something you only carry out as a sense of duty. If you can't think of any particular exercise you enjoy, think back to when you were younger and probably fitter. What type of activity did you like when you were at school? What exercises did you enjoy when you were younger – perhaps you played badminton or enjoyed running?

It's important not to push yourself too hard if you're not used to taking regular exercise. It's best to start off with a few minutes of walking every day, then build up to longer periods of light exercise. If you haven't exercised for several months, or you have an underlying medical condition such as high blood pressure or diabetes, make sure you talk to your doctor first.

Use this checklist to help you get going with your new exercise routine:

- Choose an exercise that you enjoy

- Make sure that you have the right equipment and clothing

- Start with light exercises and only gradually work up to more vigorous ones

- Exercise with a friend if that suits you

- Try to exercise every day, or every other day, at the same time so you establish a routine

- If you're just starting out, reward yourself for exercising during the first two weeks

- Learn to live with disruptions to your exercise routine – if you need to take a break for a few days, go back to your exercise plan as soon as possible

It might be difficult to keep motivated to start with – if you're feeling tired, going for a run might be the last thing you want to do. But as you start to notice your fitness and tolerance levels increasing together, it will become easier and easier to find your motivation and stay on track with your exercise programme.

Some people have concerns about starting to exercise – we've listed some of these common worries, and suggested some things to think about.

If you're concerned about this ...	Think about this ...
'Exercise might bring on some of my panic symptoms'	The effects of exercise are similar to some symptoms of panic. Exercise will: • Make you feel hot and flushed • Raise your heart rate • Make you breathe harder • Make you sweat But it's important to remember that these are healthy, natural bodily responses to exercise. So although these sensations may remind you of having a panic attack, they are not anxiety-related.
'I'm hesitant about starting an exercise programme because I'm so unfit'	Try some very light exercise, like slow walking, every day. Remember that gentle, regular exercise is far better than doing none at all. As you become fitter, you'll notice that you won't get out of breath so easily, and you'll be less aware of your increased heart rate. When you feel more confident about your level of fitness, you can start to introduce more vigorous exercise into your programme.
'I'm anxious about leaving the house'	At first, this may limit the type of exercise you choose, especially if you have agoraphobia. You could ask a friend or relative to exercise with you. Or you could exercise at home until you've built up your confidence to the level where you're ready to leave the house.

Nutrition and drugs

Eating sensibly, and according to your body's needs, is a first step in combating stress and keeping you mentally healthy. If you usually eat erratically – say you skip breakfast, or you make do with fatty and sugary snacks – try to change the way you eat. Get into the habit of having nutritious meals, or eating healthy snacks at regular intervals. This avoids wide swings in the level of sugar in your blood – major fluctuations can produce physical symptoms similar to those you experience when you're anxious.

It's not just coffee that contains caffeine – tea, cocoa, cola drinks and chocolate also have this stimulant. If you have too much you can feel 'hyped up' and this can increase your risk of having a panic attack. Some people are especially sensitive to caffeine – they may feel jittery after just one or two cups.

Nicotine is another powerful stimulant – it can also increase your anxiety. Giving up smoking has huge benefits for both your physical and mental health. If you want to give up, but you're finding it difficult, talk to your pharmacist or doctor about it. There's plenty of support available, along with programmes designed to minimize or avoid the unpleasant withdrawal symptoms that could make your anxiety worse.

Drinking too much alcohol can also bring on panic attacks. It's a good idea to keep an eye on how much you drink – just a couple of glasses of wine with dinner each night may increase to four, five or more on a daily basis. Keeping within the limits is critical if you want to recover from panic disorder. Men should have no more than three to four units a day, while women should aim for no more than two to three units a day. (A small (125ml) glass of wine is 1.3 units, a single (25ml) measure of gin is 0.9 units, and a pint of beer is 2.3 units). It's also a good idea to have at least two to three 'alcohol-free' days per week.

Follow these tips for a healthy diet:

- Eat at least five portions of fruit and vegetables each day

- Drink plenty of fluids, especially water, throughout the day

- If you're trying to lose weight, do it gradually and avoid crash diets or fasting

- Eat regular meals and try not to go for long periods without food

- Try to limit the amount of coffee and tea you drink

- Keep your alcohol consumption below the recommended limits

- If you smoke, think about quitting – you can get help from your doctor or pharmacist

- Avoid stimulant or mood-altering drugs, unless your doctor has prescribed them

Sleep

When it comes to sleep, everyone's different, although most people need between seven and nine hours every night. Some people can make do with less, while others need more to function well. Not having enough sleep – or even having too much – can make you tired, irritable and less able to cope with the demands of the day.

There are many other differences in the way people sleep – try thinking about how you sleep:

- Some people function better in the mornings, while others are at their best in the evening – when do you concentrate best at work?

- Are you most refreshed when you've had a long stretch of unbroken sleep, or do you prefer to get up regularly to go to the bathroom or to have a drink?

- Are you a sound sleeper, or do you wake up at the slightest noise, or when the light starts to come through the curtains?

- Do you move around in your sleep or do you wake up in the same position as you fell asleep?

- Do you snore?

Sleep cycles, to some extent, are thought to be 'inbuilt'. So although it's possible to alter them substantially – say going to bed early when you're really a night owl – it's difficult to do this in the short term. It's important to realize that everyone has their own individual sleep habits. There are no fixed 'rules' about the right time to go to bed, how deep your sleep should be, or the number of hours that you need. The one thing to focus on is whether you feel refreshed when you wake up. If you don't, try looking at your sleep pattern more closely. For example:

- Do you have difficulty falling asleep or staying asleep?

- Do you suffer from repeated nightmares or sudden awakenings at night?

- Do you wake too early in the morning?

If you've answered 'yes' to any of these questions, you might find it useful to keep a 'sleep diary', which will help you pinpoint any problems. There's an example of a sleep diary below, and a blank one for you to use (there is another blank one at the back of the workbook should you need it). When you wake up each morning write down how refreshed you feel using a scale of '0' to '10', where:

- '0' is 'extremely unrefreshed'

- '10' is 'very refreshed'

- Use the final column to jot down notes about any problem areas so that you can work out how to improve the quality of your sleep.

Example of a sleep diary

Date	Sleep rating	Problem area(s)
June 3	6	Awakened by a loud storm outside; afraid of thunder and lightning
June 4	4	Had too much to drink the night before
June 5	2	Worried about work, couldn't fall asleep

Sleep Diary

Date	Sleep rating	Problem area(s)

There are some basic strategies you can use to improve your chances of getting a good night's sleep. You may have already discovered your own way of making sure you wake up refreshed, but here are some of the more common remedies you can try just before you go to bed:

- Avoid any vigorous activity or tasks where you need to concentrate intensely (for at least two hours before you go to bed)

- Have a warm bath or shower to help you relax

- Drink a glass of warm milk (not coffee)

- Try to avoid alcohol

- Listen to music or do something relaxing such as reading a book (but perhaps not a thriller!)

- Try to 'switch off' from the day's worries and stresses: promise yourself that you'll think about them the next morning

- Use a relaxation exercise or tape (see the section on 'Relaxation'.)

Relaxation

It's important to take time to relax and enjoy yourself. Try to put aside some time every week to do something you enjoy – whether it's an exercise class, meditation or yoga, seeing a film or meeting up with friends. Doing something you enjoy is a great way to distract yourself from your everyday worries, unwind and recharge your batteries.

You may like to have some relaxation time every day, or you might prefer to save up all of your leisure time for the weekend. Whatever you do, it's important to make it a priority – try not to let a busy workload or other commitments eat into the time you've set aside for yourself.

When you choose activities to help you relax, make sure they really are ones you enjoy, and that you're not simply doing something to please someone else. Use the space below to list some of the things you enjoy doing to relax. They may be things you haven't done for a while, things you sometimes already do, or activities you've often thought you'd like to do one day.

Relaxing activities	*How often do you do them*
1	
2	
3	
4	
5	
6	
7	
8	

Another way to relax is to use a technique called progressive muscle relaxation. If you practise this exercise regularly it will help to reduce muscle tension and other symptoms of stress. The technique involves progressively tensing and relaxing the major groups of muscles in your body, while you breathe slowly and steadily. You need to practise the technique at least once a day to feel the benefits, and doing it twice a day is even better. There are detailed instructions for the exercise, below.

You'll probably begin to feel the benefits after two to three weeks of regular practice. Before you start practising, think about what time of day will fit best with your routine – for instance it can be a good idea to put aside some time when you first wake up in the morning, and again before you go to sleep at night. You can use the self-monitoring form at the end of this section to remind yourself to practise regularly. There is an extra form at the end of the book if you need it.

You can also buy relaxation cassette tapes and compact discs to help you to learn the technique. If you use one of these, try practising without it as well so that you can perform the exercises independently. This is handy in case you go away on holiday, or you need to practise the relaxation exercise when you don't have your tape or compact disc with you.

Once you've mastered the technique, you can try doing a mini-relaxation exercise when you don't have time to do the full exercise – for instance on a bus or a train. With practice, this mini-relaxation exercise can be almost as effective as the full-scale method.

Progressive Muscle Relaxation – full relaxation exercise

- Find a comfortable, quiet place to sit or lie down, and try to make sure that you won't be interrupted for about twenty minutes. You may need to tell the people you live with that you don't want to be disturbed, or you could organize time to be alone in a quiet room.

- Close your eyes and focus on your breathing, keeping it slow and even. Say the word 'relax' to yourself a few times as you breathe out.

- Tense your right foot, squeezing your toes together and pointing them downwards. Focus on that tension. Slowly release the tension as you breathe out, saying the word 'relax' to yourself.

- Now tense your right calf muscle and hold the tension for a while. Slowly release the tension as you breathe out.

- Progress through your body, working through the muscles of your right leg, left leg, buttocks, back, abdomen, chest, shoulders, left arm, left hand and fingers, right arm, right hand and fingers, neck, jaw, lips, eyes, and forehead, tensing and relaxing each group of muscles in the same way.

- Scan through your body and make sure that most of the tension has been released. If some areas are still tense, spend extra time relaxing those muscles.

- Slowly open your eyes. Try to maintain that feeling of relaxation for the rest of the day; or, if it's the evening, keep hold of the feeling as you go to bed and prepare for sleep.

Progressive Muscle Relaxation – mini-relaxation exercise:

- Close your eyes   • Practise your slow breathing   • Mentally say 'relax'

- Gently tense and relax the muscles of either your hands or feet

Use the chart on the next page to monitor your daily muscle relaxation exercises and feel free to use the additional sheet at the back of this workbook should you need it. Use a scale of '0' to '10', where:

- '0' is 'not at all effective'

- '10' is 'very effective'

Daily muscle relaxation exercises

Time of day	Monday	Tuesday	Wednesday	Thursday	Friday	Saturday	Sunday
Morning effectiveness rating							
Comments							
Evening effectiveness rating							
Comments							

Summary

Review of Step 2

In Step 2 you looked at ways to improve your physical health and reduce your vulnerability to stress. Now that you've read the chapter, try to answer the following questions about your current lifestyle and how you think you could improve it:

1 Are you currently doing any regular exercise? If not, what types of exercise could you start doing on a regular basis?

2 Have you got a good diet? Are you eating regular meals? Have you reduced your intake of coffee, tea and chocolate? Are you on a programme to stop smoking? Have you reduced the amount of alcohol you drink?

3 Do you find it difficult to fall asleep and/or stay asleep? Are you waking up too early? What can you do to improve your sleep?

4 Do you give yourself enough time for relaxation and recreation? If not, how can you reorganize your schedule so that you can make more time?

Summary continues on next page

Summary

5 When can you practise the progressive muscle relaxation exercises? How are you going to make sure that you practise them at least once, and preferably twice, a day?

Remember

- Changing your lifestyle so that it becomes less stressful might take several weeks or even months, and you may come up against several barriers to making these changes. But if you start with small changes, the larger ones won't seem so threatening or overwhelming.
- Make sure that you're not attempting to change too many aspects of your lifestyle too quickly, and accept that there are likely to be interruptions and distractions. The important message is to treat any setbacks as temporary and get back on track with the course as soon as possible.

SECTION 4: Step 3 – Controlling Your Panic Attacks

This section will help you understand:

- How to control overbreathing or hyperventilation

- How to use distraction techniques

- How to put together a package of coping techniques for your panic attacks

In Step 2 you looked at ways of reducing your overall stress levels by making changes to your lifestyle. By being active, eating well and improving the quality of your sleep and relaxation time, you can reduce your vulnerability to stress symptoms and panic attacks. Making these changes can take time, so continue with your programme to improve your lifestyle at the same time as you begin to practise specific exercises to combat symptoms of panic.

Like any new skill, it might take quite a bit of time and practice to learn how to control your panic attacks, and become confident using the techniques. But if you gain control of your panic symptoms, you'll be able to start doing the things that you may have been avoiding because you're worried they'll set off a panic attack. This can have a positive knock-on effect – it may help you feel better physically, which can be the start of a positive cycle away from stress and anxiety.

Step 3 shows you specific ways to control symptoms of panic. You might already be using some of these techniques, while others may be completely new to you. If you practise these techniques regularly, you'll equip yourself with the tools to prevent the debilitating symptoms of panic and you'll be able to control minor symptoms of anxiety.

Ways to control overbreathing or hyperventilation

It's normal to breathe faster in certain situations – for instance, when you've got a fever, you've been exercising or you've experienced a sudden shock. But some people develop a habit of overbreathing (hyperventilation) when they're stressed or worried. If you're susceptible, overbreathing itself can trigger a panic attack (see Part

One Section 3). Once you start to have a panic attack, it becomes difficult to breathe, or your breathing becomes irregular, and the 'hyperventilation-panic' cycle begins.

Hyperventilation is thought to cause unpleasant physical sensations by changing the balance of gases in your bloodstream. But by simply slowing your breathing rate, you can increase the amount of carbon dioxide in your blood and reverse these unwelcome effects. So by reversing the process of hyperventilation, you'll find yourself feeling less aroused, less anxious and you'll be less likely to experience symptoms of panic.

We're going to focus on two possible ways to prevent a panic attack by increasing the amount of carbon dioxide in your bloodstream. Try using these techniques individually, and in combination, to control your panic attacks – see what works best for you.

Slow breathing

You can use this technique anywhere and it only takes a few minutes. The aim of the exercise is to slow your breathing rate to about eight to 10 breaths a minute when you feel anxious or panicky. If you practise the exercise regularly, and learn to keep your normal breathing rate at the correct level, you'll find it easier to control your breathing when you notice the early symptoms of panic.

- Begin by focusing your attention on your breathing. Try not to control your breathing rate just yet, but concentrate on the sensation of breathing. If your mind wanders off to other things, gently bring back your attention to your breathing.

- Practise 'abdominal' breathing. Place one hand over your stomach and gently expand the muscles in that region every time you breathe in, so that your stomach expands outwards. At the same time, try to reduce any movement in your chest and shoulders when you breathe. If necessary, watch yourself in the mirror to make sure that your shoulders hardly move. This technique stops you from taking gasping, sharp breaths.

- Now, on your next breath in, hold your breath to the count of 10 (for 10 seconds). Do not take an excessively deep breath before you hold your breath. If you find this too difficult, try holding your breath to the count of eight.

- Now, breathe out slowly.

- Now breathe in to the slow count of three and then out to the slow count of three. Keep breathing in and out to the count of three, trying not to take overly-deep breaths. Try pacing your breathing so that it takes three seconds to breathe in and three seconds to breathe out.

- Carry on breathing at this rate for at least one minute.

- If you still feel panicky, hold your breath for a further 10 seconds and repeat the exercise. Continue practising the exercise until the sensations of panic subside.

If you practise this exercise regularly and frequently – five or six times a day – you'll find that you can control your breathing all of the time. Turn it into a secret 'game' you play on the bus, at traffic lights, or whenever you have an idle moment. With practice you'll be able to use this exercise to control panicky sensations before they turn into full-blown panic attacks.

The paper bag technique

This method of controlling overbreathing involves breathing from a paper bag and it doesn't take as much practice as slow breathing. It's thought to increase the amount of carbon dioxide in your bloodstream by simply restricting the amount of oxygen you breathe in. At the same time, it increases your intake of carbon dioxide as you breathe back in the air that you've already exhaled. Don't worry – you'll still absorb enough oxygen!

- When you feel panicky, open up a small paper bag and place it over your mouth and nose. Keep the bag firmly in place by holding it close to your face with your hands. Try not to allow any gaps where air can escape.

- Now breathe slowly and regularly into the bag. Keep breathing in and out into the bag until the panic attack begins to subside and your breathing becomes easy.

- If you don't have a bag at hand, you can improvise by cupping your hands around your nose and mouth and breathing slowly.

If you find this technique works for you, start carrying a paper bag with you in your handbag or pocket, so you don't have to worry about finding one in a hurry. If you're in public, the handcupping technique can be more convenient and less obtrusive – and you might prefer to do this if you feel more anxious when people look at you. But if you can find a private place, the paper bag technique will help you restore the balance of gases in your blood quickly and help to control your anxiety.

Distraction techniques

When you're having a panic attack, it might seem almost impossible to think about anything else except your symptoms. But if you focus on your symptoms it usually makes them worse and increases the severity of the panic attack. If you can learn to focus your attention on something else, it can help to reduce your panic.

There are a number of techniques you can try to help take your mind off the sensations of panic – you may have already found some of your own. Here are three techniques that many people find useful to control their panic symptoms – try all of them and see which works best for you.

1 **Counting** Some people find that if they focus on counting objects around them, they can distract themselves from an imminent panic attack. You could count the number of red cars passing by on the road or the number of windows in a building. Or you could multiply numbers in your mind. It doesn't matter what you count – so long as you focus on the counting rather than your panic symptoms. It doesn't matter if you become distracted and lose count – just start again.

2 **Visualizing** It can be relaxing to imagine yourself in a pleasant or enjoyable setting, away from the cares of daily life. When you begin to experience the early signs of anxiety, try imagining a pleasant scene from your memory, or from a movie or book. For example, try visualizing a warm sunny day at the beach, or a walk through a beautiful park. Think of a scene that is special for you alone, and try to make the details as real as possible – think in turn about the sounds you can hear in the scene, the smells and the colours. If you practise the same scene over and over, it will help you slip into it more easily when you need to use it.

3 **Intellectualizing** Another method to distract yourself is to 'intellectualize' the symptoms of panic by acknowledging the symptoms in an objective manner. For example, while you feel anxious you can note down all the symptoms and fears you're experiencing and rate their severity. This technique might suit you best if you're good at stepping back from yourself and your anxieties to 'self-examine' and record your experiences. The panic attack becomes an external 'thing' that you can examine from a distance – as if you're watching and rating a film – rather than something that's inside you, controlling you.

You may also find that simple, everyday activities like talking to a friend on the telephone, looking at pictures in a magazine or scrapbook, listening to the radio or watching television can also help to distract you from your panic sensations.

'Going with the flow'

This technique is becoming more popular and, as the name suggests, you 'go with the flow' of the panic sensations until they come to an end. Unlike distraction strategies, which encourage you to think about something else to take your mind off your panic, this technique encourages you to actually focus on the physical sensation of panic. If you focus on these sensations until your panic attack subsides, it will make you more confident that your anxiety will eventually dissipate and that nothing bad will actually happen – such as 'going crazy', fainting or having a heart attack.

Putting together a package of coping techniques

It's important to learn which techniques work best for you when you feel anxious, so that you've got the best toolkit to help you face difficult situations. Simply knowing that you've got a set of tried and trusted techniques that can help you combat *your* anxiety can give you extra confidence.

To help you decide which distraction techniques work best for you, make a list of the ones you've tried and think about how effective they were. Give each of them a rating from '0' to '10', where:

- '0' is 'not at all effective'

- '10' is 'very effective'

Deciding which distraction technique works best for you		
Distraction technique	Rating	Notes – e.g. when did you use the technique?

You might find it helpful to write down all the techniques that help you to control your panic attacks, perhaps on a card, which you can carry around in your purse or wallet. When you feel anxious or panicky you can take a quick look at the card to remind yourself what to do, without having to think about what's worked in the past. Here are some examples of the instructions you could write on a small card:

- Hold breath for ten seconds
- Do slow breathing exercise
- Focus attention on counting technique

- Put paper bag over nose and mouth
- Breathe slowly
- Visualize peaceful scene

- Focus on physical sensations
- Rate the level of anxiety on a '0' to '10' scale
- Let the sensations of panic wash over you
- Allow yourself time to recover from the panic attack

Once you begin to feel the panic attack subsiding, try to remain where you are and continue what you were doing, but at a slower pace. For example, if you have a panic attack in the shopping centre, try to stay there for a while after the attack has subsided, even if you only walk around slowly rather than do any shopping. If you escape from a situation because you've had a panic attack, it can make it difficult to go back to that situation later. Try to reward yourself for coping with the panic attack – treat yourself to something such as buying some nice toiletries or phoning a friend – and remember to praise yourself for handling the event as well as you did.

In Part Three, you will continue the six-step self-help course and learn how to challenge unhelpful thinking styles and deal with the physical sensations often associated with panic. You'll also be helped to overcome agoraphobia. You'll learn to troubleshoot problem areas and the best way to avoid and, if necessary, get over any setbacks.

Summary

Review of Step 3

Step 3 has shown you some important techniques for preventing and controlling panic attacks. If you practise these techniques regularly, you'll be better able to overcome symptoms of panic and to start doing the things that you may have been avoiding.

There will probably still be times when you experience symptoms of anxiety, even though you're practising these skills. But it's quite normal to expect the occasional panic attack or anxiety symptom while you're recovering from panic disorder. If this happens, try to see your anxiety or panic attack as a minor setback that simply gives you the opportunity for more practice. It's important to keep telling yourself that you're on the path to recovery and that the occasional slip along the way doesn't mean that you're falling back to the beginning.

Ask yourself the following questions to review your progress in Step 3 (circle 'yes' or 'no' for each question, where relevant):

1 Are you managing to slow down your breathing rate?

Yes   No

2 Are you practising your chosen breathing exercise regularly?

Yes   No

3 Which distraction techniques work best for you?

4 Have you written down those helpful techniques on a card, and do you use the card promptly when you need to?

Yes   No

5 Are you managing to remain in difficult situations, at least until your anxiety begins to subside?

Yes   No

When you can answer 'yes' to all of questions 1, 2, 4 and 5, you're ready to progress to the next step. Step 4 examines the thinking styles that can contribute to your anxiety and panic attacks.

Extra Charts and Worksheets

Panic attack diary

Date	Situation	Anxious symptoms (0–10)	Coping (0–10)	How I would have liked to cope

Monitoring situations or activities that you may be avoiding

Situation	Anxiety rating (0–10)

Sleep diary

Date	Sleep rating	Problem area(s)

Daily muscle relaxation exercises

Time of day	Monday	Tuesday	Wednesday	Thursday	Friday	Saturday	Sunday
Morning effectiveness rating							
Comments							
Evening effectiveness rating							
Comments							

Thoughts and Reflections